TWENTY-FIVE YEARS *to* LIFE

A Year or Two in Review

Millie Valley

NEWMAN SPRINGS PUBLISHING
320 Broad Street
Red Bank, NJ 07701

First originally published by Newman
Springs Publishing 2024

ISBN 979-8-89308-710-9 (Paperback)
ISBN 979-8-89308-711-6 (Digital)

To Craig Longo

Prologue

Circa 1979

I wrote to him.

Together,
One word that means you and me
Something we will always be.

P.S. I hope you realize you are going to be a very special part of me for the rest of my life.

And he wrote to me.

Time,
Maybe not this time or tomorrow,
Or next year or whenever,

But time and understanding and honesty
Will prove me right.

You are part of me
And will be a part of me forever.

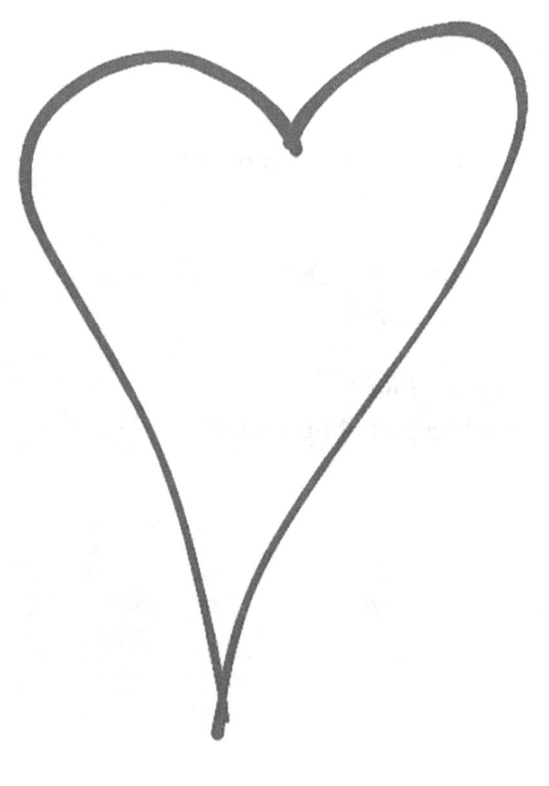

Someday (Love Long Lost)

Impossible as it may seem
Something similar to a dream.
Two hearts broken, lost and adrift
Both still waiting for the fog to lift.
A true love abandoned, left unattended
Until a silence lasting decades, suddenly ended.

Two old lovers standing face-to-face
A dreamlike moment ends in an embrace.
Endless heartache slowly melts away
With hope for another shared special day.
And maybe someday to reunite
Turning a love gone wrong, right.

Somewhere in Time

Where has it been
Hidden so deep in my existence,
The longing for your love
Will forever be persistent.
This journey of the heart
Will find its destination
Somewhere in time.

So Glad

Hello old lover, hello old friend
So glad to talk to you again.

My heart's been aching, my love's been waiting
To talk to you again.

The silence broke, there still is hope
So glad to talk to you again.

I'm with another, you found a lover
But still so glad to talk to you again.

My wish is this, to find what we missed
And not just talk to you again.

Again

Just put your hand in mine
To recreate that time
When I'd look into your eyes
And feel the highest of highs.

Yes put your hand in mine
Let's make it work this time
It was so right before
And all I want is much more.

'Cause if you put your hand in mine
Maybe we could just slow down time
To extend the years
From those lost to tears.

So put your hand in mine
It's just a matter of time
Can we try this again
Will you please be my best friend.

Midsummer's Eve

Circle left to turn back time.
One year tomorrow is still on my mind.
Remembering then,
Remembering when,
The love of my life
Was my most intimate friend.

Coffee Time

Since our last coffee
I think of you perpetually
Morning, noon, and night literally
You are always on my mind.

It's been tough since our last coffee
But it is what it is
And I live with that
While I yearn for our next coffee.

Your Words

Your words are so powerful you see
Your words they speak to me
I want to fill my day
Listening to everything you say
What you say in such a powerful way
Each and every day.

Tell Me One Thing

Tell me one thing.
Tell me one thing about your life today.
Tell me one thing that helps you get through the day.
Tell me one thing each and every day.

Tell me one thing.
Tell me one thing you didn't want to say.
Tell me one thing that made us lose our way.
Tell me one thing each and every day.

Tell me one thing.
Tell me one thing that I didn't know.
Tell me one thing you were afraid to show.
Tell me one thing each and every day.

Tell me one thing.
Tell me one thing that I don't want to hear.
Tell me one thing that I've always feared.
Tell me one thing each and every day.

Tell me one thing.
Tell me one thing that you feel today.
Tell me one thing that will make me stay.
Tell me one thing each and every day.

Tell Me One Thing
Each and Every Day

Tell me one thing about your life today.
Tell me one thing that helps you through the day.
Tell me one thing. Tell me one thing.

Tell me one thing you really feel today.
Tell me one thing that will make me stay away.
Tell me one thing. Tell me one thing each and every day.

Yes (In Closing)

Yes, I have another.
And yes, you found a lover.
Yes, I made a life.
And yes, you have a wife.
Yes, he loves me.
And yes, she loves you.
So I guess there is nothing left for us to do.
The facts are clear.
It is as I feared.
We are to be separated for life.

Who Knew...
A Year in Review

A unique perspective developing before my eyes
My child becomes a man while sifting through much
     hypocrisy and lies.
And the couple I've watched for the last fifty years
Starts unraveling amid so many aging fears.
All still holding on to family and home
With the hope they will never find themselves alone.
As for me...

As for Me

Seeing you contributed to a very difficult time.
I lost my way and couldn't say all that was on my
    mind.
I'm ready now to express how you really let me down.
It wasn't all you I know that is true.
I accept the blame that is due, but there are a few
    answers I wish I knew.
Like what in the world did we get ourselves into.
I'm a prisoner now with no way out and with no one
    to blame but myself.
Being trapped with another was tough enough.
Then reconnecting with you,
I just didn't know what to do
As I relived all those past feelings
In a yearlong solitude.
Now I've finally regained my senses
And started thinking things through.
I'm breaking down some of those old fences
And making my way back to you.

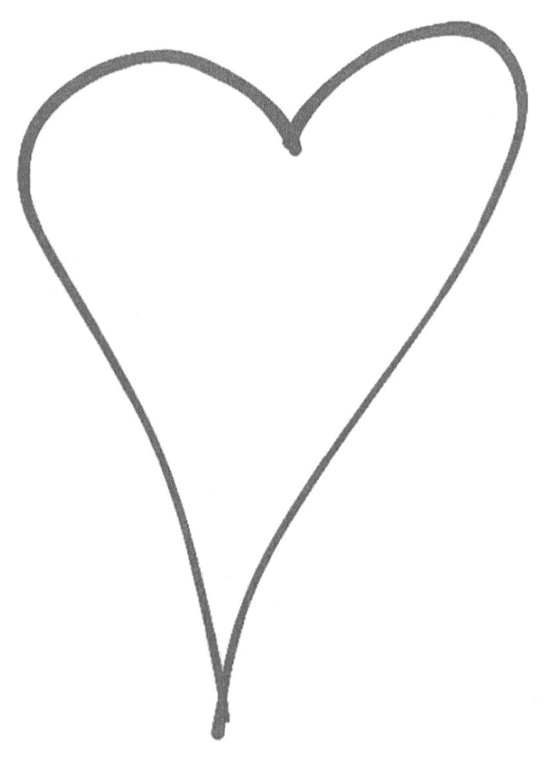

Twenty-Five Years to Life

Impossible as it may seem something similar to a dream.
After decades of silence, two old lovers find them-
  selves reunited in a seemingly timeless embrace.
They love each other, Lord, you can see that it's true.
With eyes locked and motionless, both aware of the great
  impact this moment would have on their lives.
Trouble ahead, trouble behind.
After so many years of living in the past, the One
  finally found a wife and made a life. The Other
  burying deep emotions, abandoned true love
  and started a family with another.
The One watched from a distance.
My eyes adored you.
The Other cried through the night.
Sometimes when we touch.
The One found closure while the Other lost her way…
And maybe someday to reunite, turning a love gone
  wrong right.

On That Same Day

Do you remember the time?
Do you remember the date?
It was November 24
At 11:48.
At my parents' last resting place
With their deaths still so hard to face.
I was protesting, feeling such sorrow
When I found myself confessing what they already knew
Announcing my unending love for you and only you.
I wondered right away
When you later sent the picture of your father's grave
If on that same day
Were we both crying about our loss
If on that same day
We were both feeling such remorse.

I, too, took a picture that day
The place their names would always stay
The place I still keep forgetting to pray
I wonder, Was it the same day?
Were we both drawn to those two places
To those three people who deep down inside
Wished us both only happiness, for that they always
     tried.
To the only three people who always wished us noth-
     ing but good.
And where our true love will always be completely
     and totally understood.

With You

Until I'm living in the moment with you
I will always be thinking of you
Dreaming of what we will do
When I'm living in the moment with you.

Sunsetters

A cross country adventure. An imaginary journey of
    the heart.

Sharing tales from long lost years,
Dreaming of moments filled with laughter,
Listening to each other's deep dark fears,
Regretting the unstoppable tears that came after,

From the emotional highs to the overwhelming lows,
A finite linear adventure between two intimate friends,
A fantastic fantasy to weave not too difficult to conceive,
With no true beginning or end,

The start is a familiar place, lost and alone,
Patiently waiting for the moment both can embrace,
Seeking the courage to face
A shared hope that was lost in space,

To be united as one, live a loving life and just have fun,
Watch the sun rise in the east
And together experience the sun set in the west
When the journey is done.

Star-Crossed Lovers, You and Me

Living on memories of you
Nothing left for us to do
I've deeply loved you from day one
Every day was so much fun
I fill my days with thoughts of you
Nothing else we can do
Star-crossed lovers, you and me
Star-crossed lovers, we will always be
When I was off, you were on
When I was ready, you were gone
Star-crossed lovers for eternity

Fault Lines

What a blur
What a blunder.
Separated for years
One can only wonder.

Faults and foolishness
Who knows why.
Lost for decades
One can only sigh.

Storm Front

The day, you say, the music struck you
That very morning, I awoke to something new
That something swept over me and must have hit
      you too.
It verified what was already known to you and me
We are truly connected, and our lives have been
      deeply affected.

Our reunion, for me, brought much confusion, you see.
Confusion, I say, until that very day
The day an emotional storm front came rolling through.
The day a musical lightning bolt hit you.
A tempest's end that was well overdue.

On that same day, my thoughts of you did clear
While close to my heart, all those feelings remain dear.
No more perpetual delusions or fear
A lingering storm of two plus years
Just vanished, completely disappeared…how weird.

Until Now

Until now
There was such fear
Until now
Nothing was clear
Until now
I'd shed a tear
Until now

Don't Look Now

I've devised an exercise that we can do for fun
Go outside, and I will too at one o'clock every Sunday
    afternoon
Let's close our eyes and face the sun
Let's feel its warmth as we become one

7, 8, 9

8, 9, 10
Code you chose to send.

8, 9, 10
Brings us here together again.

8, 9, 10
Does it mean we have reached the end?

8, 9, 10
Let's work backward instead my friend.

The End

The end will be our beginning.
The end will be a fresh start.
The end will be the first inning.
The end will mend the heart.

Epilogue

He wrote to me more recently.

The day I awoke and read your poems
The feelings within me grew.

Every page so full of us
When passion and love were new.

The words you wrote, so perfectly placed
Each one to me so true.

Somewhere in time, we melted together
Becoming one, me-you.

Passion and love and unspoken words
Gifted to so very few.

One year together

Together:
    One word that means you and me.
    Something that we'll always be.
Let's stay Together.....Forever!
        I Love you.